Why Living Things Need...

Water

Daniel Nunn

Heinemann Library
Chicago, Illinois

www.capstonepub.com
Visit our website to find out more information about Heinemann-Raintree books.

To order:
☎ Phone 888-454-2279
💻 Visit www.capstonepub.com to browse our catalog and order online.

Edited by Dan Nunn, Rebecca Rissman, and Sian Smith
Designed by Joanna Hinton-Malivoire
Picture research by Ruth Blair
Production by Victoria Fitzgerald
Originated by Capstone Global Library Ltd
Printed and bound in the United States of America.
756

Library of Congress Cataloging-in-Publication Data
Nunn, Daniel.
  Water / Daniel Nunn.—1st ed.
    p. cm.—(Why living things need)
  Includes bibliographical references and index.
  ISBN 978-1-4329-5917-3 (hb)—ISBN 978-1-4329-5923-4 (pb)
1. Water—Juvenile literature. I. Title.
  GB662.3.N86 2012
  553.7—dc22   2011014651

Acknowledgments
We would like to thank the following for permission to reproduce photographs: Alamy: Ann & Steve Toon/Robert Harding World Imagery, 17, Dave King/Dorling Kindersley, 11, Micheko Productions, Inh. Michele Vitucci, 6; Getty Images: Ariel Skelley/Blend Images, 21, Peter Dazeley, 14, Tetra Images, 7, Zak Kendal, 16; Shutterstock: beerkoff, 18, CHAINFOTO24, 20, Dean Mitchell, 8, ESB Professional, 5, evan66, 15, Gyuszko-Photo, back cover, 19, Johan Swanepoel, cover, Levent Konuk, 22 bottom left, Ludmila Yilmaz, 22 right, Nicky J Graham, 9, Pressmaster, 4, 23 top, ronstik, 11 Inset, 23 bottom, Specta, 13, Villiers Steyn, 10, 23 middle, Voyagerix, 22 top left, Willyam Bradberry , 12

We would like to thank Nancy Harris, Dee Reid, and Diana Bentley for their assistance in the preparation of this book.

Contents

What Is Water?

Water is a liquid. Liquids are runny.

Water has no smell, color, or taste.

cloud

Water falls from the clouds as rain.

Rain fills up rivers, lakes, and oceans.

Living Things and Water

People, other animals, and plants are living things.

All living things need water.

Animals drink water through their mouths.

roots

Plants take in water through
their roots.

Some living things live in water.

Fish live in water.

Why Do Living Things Need Water?

People and other animals need water to stay alive.

Plants need water to stay alive, too.

People need water to keep their
bodies working.

Other animals need water to keep their bodies working, too.

Plants need water, air, and sunlight to make food.

Plants need water to grow.

Some living things use water to keep clean.

People use water to keep clean.

Water Quiz

Which of these things does not need water?

Answer on page 24

Picture Glossary

liquid something runny that you can pour, such as water or milk

living thing something that is alive, such as an animal or a plant

roots the part of a plant that holds it in the ground. Roots bring water to the plant.

Index

Answer to question on page 22
The fish and the tiger need water.
The books do not need water.

Notes for parents and teachers

Before reading

Take in a jug of water and show the children how you can easily pour the water into another container. Explain that water is a liquid and is runny. Can they think of another liquid that they can drink that is runny? Pass the water around and ask the children if it has a smell. Does it have a color? Ask the children to take a small mouthful of water from their own water containers and ask if they think it has a taste. Explain that all living things need water to stay alive.

After reading

• Set up an area where small groups can pour water from one container to another. Ask them why they can do this. Encourage the use of vocabulary such as "liquid" and "runny."

• Provide two small potted plants. Explain that one plant will be given a little water every day but the other plant will not get any water. At the end of the week show the children the plants and ask them what has happened. With the help of the children, write up the experiment onto a large sheet of paper. Ask two children to illustrate the results.